# Reiki

*(The Definitive Guide)*

*Increase Energy, Improve Health and Feel Great with Reiki Healing*

# Table of Contents

Introduction

Chapter 1: Getting Started with Reiki

Chapter 2: The Benefits of Reiki Energy

Chapter 3: Reiki Principles and Symbols

Chapter 4: Traditional vs. Western Reiki

Chapter 5: Reiki: The 3 Pillars

Chapter 6: Reiki and Chakras

Chapter 7: Reiki Basic Hand Positions

Chapter 8: Breathing Techniques for Reiki

Chapter 9: Using Crystals with Reiki

Chapter 10: Strengthening Reiki Energy

Chapter 11: Reiki in Everyday Life

Conclusion

# Introduction

Reiki, a popular holistic healing approach, actually comes from two combined Japanese words, rei and ki, which means universal life force. This traditional healing technique involves the laying on of hands and utilizes life force energy as a means of healing various ailments and balancing the body's subtle energies.

One thing that makes Reiki so popular at present is its ability to address mental, spiritual, emotional and physical imbalances. This kind of healing technique works as an effective delivery system. What a Reiki practitioner will do is that he will act as the vessel that will supply healing energies to any part of your body that need them the most. The energies will flow from the body of the practitioner through his palms while he touches the body of the patient.

The best Reiki session can help you relax. The primary reason is that it is conducted in a relaxing environment. Reiki practitioners make it a point to create a soothing environment for their clients. They set a relaxing mood with the help of meditative music, dimmed lights and bubbling music fountains. To be able to gain the best results out of Reiki, it is necessary to do it in a quiet place without distractions of any kind.

Reiki is capable of healing almost all aspects of your life. It can deal with all kinds of imbalances, can relieve stress and help bring out the best out of you. It can also boost your energy, improve your overall health and well-being and help you accept who you are, thereby allowing you to feel great about yourself. With its ability to balance all areas of your life, it would be easier for you to bring out the best out of your health and your life.

If you are interested to know more about Reiki healing and use it to improve all aspects of your life, then this book is for you. It walks you through everything that this traditional healing technique is all about: from how to get started to its principles and symbols. You will also get to know about the benefits of Reiki healing through this book.

You will also learn about its pillars, how Reiki is related to your chakras and some of the most effective Reiki hand positions and breathing techniques. This book will serve as your guide to make the most out of undergoing the Reiki healing procedure. You will know exactly what you need to do to gain most, if not all, of the benefits of Reiki through this book.

# Chapter 1: Getting Started with Reiki

Reiki refers to a spiritual and complementary healing approach that requires practitioners to lay their hands lightly above or on a person while aiming to facilitate his own healing response. The main principle of Reiki is based upon the belief that an energy is capable of supporting the natural or innate healing abilities of the body. Note, however, that contrary to what others believe, the procedure does not have any connection to a specific religious practice.

It is not also a form of massage. It is actually an effective and subtle form of energy work, which utilizes spiritually-guided life force energy. Some studies show that Reiki is capable of healing a number of conditions including fatigue, depression, anxiety and pain.

Reiki is actually the life energy which flows through humans and other living things. According to Reiki practitioners, all people are capable of connecting with their healing energies. They can even use this energy to strengthen themselves and others. This healing technique also believes that the energy or "ki" of a person is free flowing and strong. Strengthening this ki will result to a positive state of health. Blocked or weak ki or energy can trigger symptoms of emotional and physical imbalance.

One thing that makes Reiki sessions beneficial is its ability to ease your stress and tension. It also facilitates healing in various levels and aspects of your life, including emotional, physical and mental. You will also have a relaxing and pleasant experience when undergoing each session.

# What to Expect from a Reiki Healing Session?

A Reiki healing session usually takes sixty to ninety minutes. The first step is an initial session wherein you and the Reiki practitioner will discuss things related to your condition, as well as what to expect from the procedure. You can expect the practitioner to give you an idea about what will happen before, during and after the session. The initial session also gives you the chance to talk about the specific issues or problems that you are experiencing and the things you want to achieve from the procedure.

The actual Reiki healing session is conducted either through hands-on technique, wherein the practitioner will lightly touch certain parts of your body, or hands-off technique, wherein the practitioner will hold his hands slightly above certain parts of your body. In case, you do not want to be touched, make sure to tell the practitioner about it during the initial session.

During the session, you may experience a tingling or warming sensation. You may also get sheer relaxation from a comfortable position while the practitioner works on healing the different parts of your body. Most of those who undergo Reiki on a regular basis say that they have an invigorating, relaxing and pleasant experience after each session.

In the next chapters, you will get to know more about the benefits of Reiki and the different tips and techniques that will allow you to maximize the results out of each session.

# Chapter 2: The Benefits of Reiki Energy

Reiki is one of just a few natural and holistic approaches to healing that offer numerous health benefits. The good thing about Reiki is that despite being just a simple process, it still delivers profound effects. Aside from healing diseases, Reiki also works in promoting a healthy body and a positive mind so those who undergo it regularly can experience joy and satisfaction in life. This chapter will talk about some of the many benefits of applying Reiki energy into your life.

## Promotes relaxation and stress relief

One of the many things that Reiki can do is offer utmost relaxation and stress relief. This benefit stimulates the natural healing abilities of the body, including its immune functions. The fact that Reiki promotes utmost relaxation can also help improve the quality of your sleep and your present health condition. You can expect this holistic healing approach to bring inner harmony and peace. This inner harmony and peace is also valuable in achieving spiritual growth.

## Balances your mind and emotions

Reiki healing is also beneficial because it balances your mind and your emotions. Attending regular Reiki sessions can help bring out a more peaceful and calmer state of being. This can improve your ability to deal with daily stress. The mental balance that you can gain from this technique also works in enhancing your mental clarity, memory and learning ability.

Reiki is also capable of healing your emotional and mental wounds. It works through any bodily, emotional and mental dysfunctions that you are currently experiencing. The healing technique is even capable of dealing with more severe cases that require the immediate alleviation of mood swings, frustration, extreme anger and fear. The ability of Reiki to stimulate the right mental and emotional balance is also useful in strengthening and healing personal relationships.

Each session aids in improving your ability to love. It can also make you more open to the people around you, thereby allowing you to make your relationships grow. It improves your ability to empathize with others, so expect to be able to connect with others in a deeper level.

## Alleviates sorrow and emotional distress

You can also try Reiki if you want to gain immediate relief from sorrow and emotional distress. One session is already enough to help you cope with the process of grieving. It aids in cleaning and clearing up your emotions, thereby preventing you from being too drained from the negative experience. It can also offer a newer, fresher and more positive perspective about life.

## Offers relief against pain and other physical ailments

If you have been complaining about pain from arthritis, migraine, sciatica and any other painful conditions, then consider undergoing a Reiki session and find out if it works well in relieving such ailments. Some of those who tried this treatment say that they were able to experience relief from pain and other physical ailments. Reiki can also deal with symptoms of chronic fatigue, asthma, insomnia and menopause. Other conditions that Reiki can treat include ulcers, skin conditions, colds and flu, back problems, depression, anxiety and low confidence or self-esteem.

## Other Reiki Healing Benefits

Aside from the above-mentioned benefits, Reiki can also promote overall healing by restoring the right balance in all aspects and levels. It directly works on your condition or health problem, instead of just relieving or masking symptoms. It helps dissolve blocked energy while also stimulating the natural balance between the body, spirit and mind.

It also boosts your energy levels, clears your mind from unwanted thoughts, improves your focus and concentration, accelerates the self-healing ability of the body and promotes better sleep. Other benefits that you will surely enjoy from regularly undergoing Reiki sessions are reduced blood pressure, better immune system, emotional cleansing, spiritual growth, improved creativity and pain relief.

# Chapter 3: Reiki Principles and Symbols

Reiki actually works under the principle that whenever there is disruption or blockage in the natural flow of your life force energy, your risk of dealing with various health and emotional problems will also increase. You will most likely experience imbalances due to various situations that occur in your life including physical or emotional trauma and injuries.

Negative feelings and thoughts can also trigger such imbalances. These include worries, fear, anger, toxicity, negative self-talk, doubt, destructive relationships and lifestyle, nutritional depletion and unhealthy expression of emotions. If you want to gain a full understanding of Reiki healing, then learning about its principles and symbols can help you a lot. This will surely let you decide how this kind of healing can benefit you.

## Reiki Principles

### Eliminate Anger

One of the most vital Reiki principles is to eliminate anger. Anger, either at your own self or at others, can develop a serious blockage in your life force energy. It is one of the most complex internal enemies. The fact that Reiki works under the principle that you should eliminate anger makes it an effective tool in removing anger blockages that accumulated within your body all throughout the years.

However, it is incapable of removing present anger that tends to occur every day. If you want Reiki to work for you, then be willing to let go of your anger. This can help bring peace of mind.

## Eliminate your Worries

Anger typically covers present and past events; worry, on the other hand, encompasses future events. Worry does not actually produce negative results, especially if you deal with it correctly. The reason is that your worries can motivate you to perform better to produce your desired output.

However, endless and unreasonable worries are already wrong for you. These worries may fill your head and may bore holes in your body and soul. With the help of Reiki, you can let go of all your worries. This promotes internal healing.

## Be grateful

Another important principle of Reiki is to be grateful of everything that life has offered to you. One of the most important elements in this Reiki principle is inner intention. Simple things like forgiving others, smiling, gratitude, saying thank you and positive words relayed to yourself and to others are already enough to improve your life and make the people around you happy. Reiki emphasizes the importance of being grateful so you can bring joy to your spirit.

## Be Honest

Reiki also emphasizes the importance of honesty. This involves honestly performing your daily work. It also involves supporting yourself and your loved ones respectably and without causing any harm to them. With Reiki, you will know how important it is to live a respectable and honorable life. This makes it really important to live your life honestly, so you can bring abundance to your soul.

## Be Kind

Reiki can also help integrate kindness into your inner being; being kind to others is actually one of the guiding principles of this old-age healing technique. This means being kind to all things that are living. These also encompass showing kindness to and honoring your parents, elders, teachers and even strangers. Kindness can actually help you spread the love, and this is what you will get from regularly undergoing Reiki sessions.

## Reiki Symbols

The symbols used in Reiki refer to sacred healing symbols that are capable of enhancing the natural flow of your life force energy. These symbols serve as the keys in opening up doors to higher level of manifestation and awareness. The symbols are actually in Japanese forms derived from Sanskrit. Many believe that Sanskrit is the mother tongue of the majority of European languages. Reiki practitioners show their clients the symbols prior to starting the attunement process.

Imprinting comes next which works by linking the shown images to the metaphysical energies represented by the symptom. The attunement process actually works in empowering the symbols so they can fulfill their purpose. This part will introduce to you the most important symbols used in Reiki, so you will know exactly what to expect from each session and what each symbol can do for you.

## Cho Ku Rei

The intention of this symbol is light switch and its purposes include promoting accelerated healing, manifestation and increased power. It also works as a healing catalyst. This is a power symbol designed to either increase or decrease power. It looks like a coil, which is designed to retract and expand. It also works in regulating the natural flow of ki energy. This symbol has a strong manifestation power, making it an excellent focusing tool in the law of attraction field.

## Sei Hei Ki

This Reiki symbol's intention is purification and its purposes include protection, emotional and mental healing and cleansing. It also represents peace and harmony. However, take note that this symbol refuses to deal with unfair outcomes. It also works as a protective shield while also offering courage to those who are disheartened. This symbol also works as a loyal friend, especially at times of struggles and difficulties.

## Hon Sha Ze Sho Nen

The intention of this symbol is timelessness. Its goals include acting as a healing karma, offering spiritual connection and encouraging distant healing. It has extension powers, making it effective in transmitting the Reiki energy even at long distances. It signifies a shape-shifter capable of slipping through space and time. It comes with an elastic texture, making it enjoyable to use when undergoing healing visualizations. This is also an effective tool for those who would like to work on or deal with their past life issues or their inner child.

## Dai Ko Myo

This symbol promotes enlightenment, oneness, healing of the soul and empowerment. It is the core of Reiki, considering the fact that it represents almost all the things that this healing technique encompasses. Dai Ko Myo is a Reiki symbol which is rarely used to achieve a specific purpose, other than reminding people that Reiki is love that is available to all.

## Raku

The main use of this symbol is on the last stage of the attunement process. Raku intends to seal and ground newly awakened energies. It signifies a striking lightning bolt drawn from the heaven down to the Earth. It also aims to align your chakras and promote hara connection and healing.

# Chapter 4: Traditional vs. Western Reiki

When planning to undergo Reiki sessions, it pays to understand the major differences between traditional and Western Reiki since this can greatly help in knowing exactly what to expect. This chapter will briefly cover both practices, so you will know their practical and cultural differences.

## The Western Reiki

One of the most popular Reiki practices is that based on Western culture. The Western practice was passed on to Hawayo Takata, a student of Mikao Usui's direct student whose name is Chujiro Hayashi. The Western practice proved to be a great success. In fact, it helped millions of those who undergo Reiki worldwide. Western Reiki primarily focuses on the technique's healing component.

Takata's first experience in practicing Reiki involved healing herself after she encountered a number of threatening conditions. This prompted her to focus on hands-on healing technique. Throughout the years, Western Reiki evolved. The practice gained a lot of additions including the application of the Tibetan healing practice.

The thing that is always unique to the Western Reiki is its primary focus on the process of healing, one-time attunement on a per level basis and certain hand positions. The practice also makes use of the chakras that serve as energetic systems. Western Reiki also typically implement guided meditations.

The Western practice of Reiki actually revolves around the principle that Western people have the tendency to search for something good within and outside of themselves. An example of this is their strong belief on the higher self. Sometimes, they feel amazing parts that reside in and out of themselves.

This makes them feel a noticeable separation between their normal and good self. If the gap between their normal and good self is too huge, then Western Reiki aims to heal it and establish the connection.

## Traditional Reiki

Traditional Reiki, on the other hand, is more on enlightenment. It is also important to note that traditional Japanese culture does not base their beliefs on original sin, higher self and powerless and weak existence. So, basically, traditional Reiki emphasizes more on achieving enlightenment in all areas of a person's life.

The practice focuses more on establishing a good lifestyle. The practitioner needs to find enlightenment and make this a part of his lifestyle, so he can achieve a more balanced life. It also works under the principle that you need to heal yourself first before you can try healing others. Traditional Reiki makes use of an energetic system unique to the Japanese, which primarily focuses on the Hara. It has five major components that are built on and connected to each other.

Traditional Reiki sessions also use traditional meditation and breathing techniques that can help you in directly accessing energy from its source, the Hara. The result is the ability to feel the strong energy that channels through you right away.

In traditional Reiki, you will also learn about mantras and symbols. Both represent specific energies. You will also need to practice the mantra in Buddhist and a chanting style as a means of developing vibrational healing sounds. You also need to practice certain attunements several times. This is necessary in strengthening your energy.

# Chapter 5: Reiki: The 3 Pillars

Aside from strictly adhering to the major principles of Reiki, the practice also has three pillars that can enhance the success of even just a single session. The three pillars will allow you to build a connection with your higher self along with the natural source of the Reiki energy. Each pillar has a unique set of attributes. Synchronizing them can result to building a deeper connection to yourself and your true intent. This chapter will cover the three pillars of the Reiki practice.

## Gassho

This pillar refers to a kind of meditation that you will need to use to center yourself before undergoing the session. All that you have to do to perform this meditation is to bring your palms together and put them in front of your chest. Close your eyes and focus on the sensations felt by the top of your fingers. It is also crucial to clear your mind of any unwanted and unnecessary thoughts. You need to relax and allow the energy to flow naturally.

## Reiji-Ho

This pillar comes from the words Reiji, which indicates the power of Reiki, and Ho, which signifies methods. What you need to do to take advantage of this pillar is to switch the energy on. You can do this by following three steps. The first step is to do the Gassho position then ask the energy to flow naturally through you. You will then ask the acquired energy to let you use it for your client. You can do so by stating something that goes similar to this line, "I ask to use this Reiki for the highest good...."

The next step is to hold your hand and position it in front of your 3rd eye. Ask for guidance so your hands will be directed to certain areas where energy is required. This is also the pillar wherein you can ask your Reiki spirit guides for guidance. Make sure to relay your requests in your head, instead of saying them aloud. It is also important to build a really strong connection with your guides.

This is the most difficult among the three pillars since it requires the practitioner to have trust in himself and in the Reiki practice. The good news is that it is possible to achieve openness and connection if you put your heart to it and genuinely ask to be connected and open.

## Chiryo

This Reiki pillar aims to achieve treatment or overall healing. You can perform it in a couch or chair depending on your preference. It starts the treatment at the crown chakra of the client. Since it involves the actual treatment, this is the stage wherein you give the Reiki session to the client.

You will have to tap into uniform treatment points and use the ones that you learned and discovered through education and experimentation. This is the most relaxing stage for the client. The good news is that you, as the practitioner, will also gain healing from the session.

The three Reiki pillars mentioned in this chapter can put you, as the practitioner, in a centered space. It makes it possible for you to build a connection with the universal energy. With the help of the three pillars, you will also be able to accept the fact that the Reiki energy is actually the one that provides healing to your client, not you.

Once you reach the last pillar, it is crucial to let go of self-centeredness and ego to allow the smooth and natural flow of Reiki energy.

# Chapter 6: Reiki and Chakras

To make the most out of a Reiki session, it is crucial to tap into your chakras. Reiki has a strong connection to your chakras because it helps heal any imbalances and blockages. In fact, the hand positions used in each session can cover and heal all the problems in your major chakras. It is important to note that your chakras have a deep connection to your physical organs, as well as the different layers found in your aura.

## Chakras Defined

Before learning about the relationship between reiki and chakras, it is important to gain a full understanding about the latter first. Chakras actually refer to the entry gates of your aura. Your physical body actually has a double, the spiritual body which contains these entry gates, your major chakras. These refer to the centres of activities that are capable of receiving, expressing and assimilating life force energy.

The right balance in your chakras is also useful in maintaining your mental, spiritual and physical health. These chakras are also responsible for transmitting and absorbing energies from and to the nature, universe, people or things or celestial entities. You have to maintain the right balance in your chakras and prevent any blockages to promote overall healing.

Numerous factors can cause a blockage or imbalance in your chakras. These include cultural conditioning, childhood experiences or traumas, emotional and physical injuries, bad habits, lack of attention and limited belief system. It is also important to note that humans can never escape from life's difficulties. The difficulties and challenges that you have experienced may cause you to develop your own coping strategies.

The problem is when the difficulties persist, your developed coping techniques will turn into chronic patterns that will psyche as defense structures and anchor in your body. You need to discover the blockages that you carry so you can determine and comprehend their meaning and source. This way, you can develop the most effective strategies and tools to achieve healing and balance.

## The Major Chakras

### 1st Chakra - The Root Chakra

This chakra refers to the spirit of life and represents survival, support and grounding. This forms your foundation and you can find it at the bottom of your spine. It symbolizes the Earth element and has a deep connection to your survival instincts. Achieving the right balance in your root chakra and preventing any blockages makes it possible for you to take better care of yourself and to stand up for your principles. This chakra is also important in your overall well-being because it can give you the presence and security that you need.

### 2nd Chakra - The Sacral Chakra

Located at the lower back and in your sexual organs and lower back, the 2nd chakra signifies spiritual health and purity. It connects deeply to your sexuality and emotions. The main function of the sacral chakra is to promote a sense of self. It helps bring out your inner child or self. It is one of the best sources of inspiration and creativity. It also works in controlling your appetite for sensation through sight, touch, taste, smell and sound. You need to remove blockages in this chakra and maintain the right balance if you want to improve your ability and willingness to accept and adapt to change, and achieve sexual fulfilment.

## 3rd Chakra - The Solar Plexus

Also called the power chakra, this chakra represents wisdom, knowledge, personal power and desire. It mainly functions by supplying energy in the form of enthusiasm, power and heat. Solar plexus also works in ruling your consciousness, your ability to make decisions, willingness, metabolism, autonomy, personal power and creative expression. The right balance in this chakra, which is also free of blockages, can help bring out your desired level of energy, spontaneity and effectiveness. It also makes it possible for you to gain awareness of the flow of the divine universe, as well as awareness of the presence of natural guidance into your life.

## 4th Chakra - The Heart

The heart chakra promotes self-acceptance, social identity, compassion and love. It also represents new beginnings. Situated at the central part of your chest, the heart chakra works by connecting your physical self or lower ego to your spiritual self or the higher soul. Aside from allowing you to feel compassion and love deeply, your heart chakra can also help bring peace into your life. The right balance makes it possible for you to offer unconditional love to yourself and to others.

## 5th Chakra - The Throat

This chakra represents your self-expression, creative identity and sound. It brings out the spirit of expression and truth. It has a strong connection to creativity, self-expression and communication. A well-balanced throat chakra encourages free communication, making it possible for you to feel happy and centered. You can also use this chakra when meditating so you can build a deeper connection with your higher guidance. It has a strong connection to inner self and allows you to connect deeply to your soul.

## 6th Chakra - The Third Eye

Also called the third eye center or brow chakra, the 6th chakra is popular for its ability to bring out your inherent psychic awareness and spirit of clarity. It symbolizes light, intuition and archetypal identity. The main purpose of this chakra is to act as the core of your inner vision. It is where you can tap into your soul knowledge and intuition. It helps in opening up your spiritual and psychic awareness faculties and comprehend your archetypal levels. Balancing this chakra can help improve your knowledge and insight on numerous things.

## 7th Chakra - The Crown Chakra

This is where your knowingness, thought and universal identity resides. It has a strong connection to your consciousness and brings out pure awareness. This chakra serves as your connection to the greater world, as well as your collective consciousness. Balancing and removing any blockages in this chakra can help improve and bring out wisdom, harmony, spiritual connection and understanding.

## Healing Chakra Imbalances and Blockages through Reiki

A single Reiki session can help deal with any imbalances and blockages in the natural flow of your energy, including those from your major chakras. With the help of Reiki, you will be able to gain well-balanced and highly functioning chakras. This is essential in your attempt to feel complete, contented and healthy. This also works in improving your vitality.

Reiki can help treat unbalanced and weakened chakra that may trigger negative consequences including restlessness, lack of energy, disconnection to your own self and depression. It is also important to note that the 7 major chakras in your body correspond to your endocrine grandular system, and this system works in effective hormone regulation and production.

By curing any problem that affects your chakras, it will be easier for the hormone production process to take place. This kind of healing is achievable if you regularly undergo Reiki sessions. This makes it possible to align your chakras to your major endocrine glands.

A Reiki session can also help fill your physical body or your endocrine glands and your chakras or your energetic body with life force energy or Ki, which is essential in creating balance. The result would be better regulation of hormones, better health and well-being and proper growth and development. It is also helpful in coping with the challenges that you face as you age and improve your ability to react to stress.

# Chapter 7: Reiki Basic Hand Positions

The simple act of positioning or placing your hands on yourself or on someone else allows the natural Reiki energy to flow automatically. A Reiki session usually involves a number of hand placements to offer healing not only to yourself, but also to others.

## 1st Position: The Face

The first position involves placing your hands over the face of the recipient. You just need to place the palms of your hands gently on the recipient's forehead. You also need to lightly cup your fingers over his eyes. In this position, you need to take extreme caution to avoid constricting his breathing patterns. Make sure to keep his airways open.

## 2nd Position: Top of the Head and the Crown

This involves wrapping the head of the recipient with your hands. Make sure that your inner wrists touch when doing this position. Your fingertips should also be able to touch the client's ears lightly.

## 3rd Position: The Back Part of the Head

This position requires gently tucking your hands beneath the head of your client. Make sure that your hands serve as a comfortable and protective cradle for your client's head. Let your hands' back relax, so you can offer ultimate healing to your client.

## 4th Position: Jawline and Chin

Let your hands surround his jawline. Your fingertips should also touch beneath his chin while you allow your hands' heel to rest gently over or close to his ears.

## 5th Position: Heart and Neck Collarbone

Allow your right hand to wrap the neck of the recipient gently or lightly. In case he is uncomfortable with this position, hovering your hand slightly over his neck would do. Position your left hand above the center of his heart. You can do this by allowing your left arm to stretch downwards.

## 6th Position: Ribcage and the Ribs

You should position your hands in the area where the upper rib cage is located. This should be directly beneath the recipient's breasts. Just keep in mind that touching private or sensitive body parts is inappropriate when performing a Reiki treatment.

## 7th Position: The Abdomen

This position requires putting your hands on your client's solar plexus or tummy. This should be right above his navel.

## 8th Position: The Pelvic Bones

This involves placing one of your hands above every pelvic bone of your client.

## 9th Position: The Shoulder Blades

This requires positioning your hands in your client's shoulder blades. The shoulder blades refer to the specific part of the body where one frequently stores his or her emotional struggles and burden. Because the shoulder blades serve as the storage area of most negative energies, you need to let your hands and palms stay there for a longer period. This is helpful in dislodging stored negative energies.

## 10th Position: The Mid-back

This hand placement requires positioning your hands in your client's middle back.

## 11th Position: The Lower Back

From the tenth position, move your hands downwards so that you can position them in the lower back.

## 12th Position: The Sacrum

The last of the most basic Reiki hand placements require you to touch the recipient's sacral region. This should complete the entire Reiki session. As a practitioner, you need to use your hands to comb your client's aura. This is necessary in removing energetic debris that was lifted from his body when he is undergoing the treatment. This is also the stage when silently requesting to transform stagnant or negative energies into positive ones, then returning them into the universe can produce better results.

Now that you are aware of the most basic Reiki hand placements or positions, you are ready to undergo the treatment and achieve the kind of healing that you have been longing for.

# Chapter 8: Breathing Techniques for Reiki

Various breathing methods and techniques play a crucial role in the success of a Reiki treatment. Performing the breathing techniques correctly is vital in achieving ultimate healing while also obtaining positive changes in energy flow. Learning about the most effective breathing techniques for Reiki will actually help you utilize the energy change process in successfully healing yourself.

Reiki makes use of deep breathing techniques. The main reason is that deep breathing promotes calmness, peace of mind and oneness with self. Such techniques are also effective in your attempt to raise your consciousness regarding your chakras and properly access them to support overall healing. Doing deep breathing techniques correctly makes it easier for you to tap universal and natural energies.

A short breath is the first form of breathing commonly utilized in a Reiki session. This is the type of breathing most people normally do. In this type of breathing, you breath through your nose then feel your upper lungs before you exhale. To make this technique work even more effectively in a Reiki session, it is advisable to perceive the process of inhaling as a form of universal energy. You should also perceive the process of exhaling as a way of releasing your pent-up negative energies.

Another form of breathing which you can use in Reiki is that which requires you to fill the lower part of your body, in the specific place where your diaphragm and stomach are located. Make sure that your belly expands when you inhale. When exhaling, allow your stomach to shrink. Since you will fill your body in this technique, many Reiki practitioners consider it as a full and complete breath. Those who regularly meditate often use this kind of breathing.

Another breathing technique that you can use in a Reiki session involves visualizing your rib cage being filled with air. This signifies a full, complete breath. Complete breathing requires you to fill your lungs first. Next is you will fill your diaphragm. The last step would be to allow your breath to expand so that it reaches your ribs. Many practitioners believe that breathing completely allows you to slow down and call natural and universal energies.

In a Reiki session, the way you breathe contributes a lot to gaining your desired success. One of the most important aspects in performing some of the most effective Reiki breathing techniques is to imagine that every breath you take has a deep connection to light. This means visualizing a light that fills your chakras with each breath. Using your mind, it is possible to direct the light to your desired location.

This is a huge help if your goal is to circulate blocked energies in your body. The breathing techniques used in a Reiki session are also ideal for those who plan to meditate regularly. Most of them involve concentrating on your breathing patterns, so achieving a relaxed state is possible.

Doing them correctly can increase your level of consciousness while also allowing universal energies to start flowing smoothly. Just make sure to practice them in a consistent and disciplined manner so you will be able to master them.

# Chapter 9: Using Crystals with Reiki

A lot of Reiki practitioners discovered that using crystals is one of the most effective ways to improve the results of their work. According to them, crystals can help boost vibrations, thereby aiding in the process of releasing blockages in the body while also sending positive vibes that promote utmost relaxation.

The crystals also offer an aid in balancing your energies and in healing. You can even expect them to work in speeding up the treatment process.

## Laying of Stones

If you want to use crystals when practicing Reiki, then it is advisable to get an idea about how the process of laying stones works. The goal of this practice is to release any spiritual, mental, emotional and etheric blockages in your being.

If you are the healer, then your role is to offer a non-judgmental, supportive and comforting experience to your clients. This can help your clients have peace of mind when they are trying to release such negative emotions. This plays a huge role in the healing and recovery process.

It is necessary to remove the crystal that you are using in case your client does not feel any discomfort from it. Stones or crystals that tend to make your clients feel good right after placing them have the tendency to change in case their body absorbs the acquired energy.

This is the main reason why you have to really work closely with your client in this aspect. You have to know exactly what he or she feels so you will be able to find out if the treatment worked for him or not.

## Balancing your Chakras by Using Crystals for Reiki Healing

An effective yet simple way of balancing your entire chakra system involves placing a crystal or stone with an appropriate color on every area. This can help boost each chakra, thereby giving each one its own vibration without the need to change the energy or the harmony of the body.

According to Reiki practitioners, proper interaction between a person's chakras and the stones can promote a healthier vibration, which supports the healing process of the affected body part.

The simple act of putting a beneficial stone on every chakra is already an effective way to develop a tonic that will tone and strengthen the system. You have to start collecting stones or crystals and lay them all out in the area where you usually perform the healing process. This makes it possible for you to see your collection clearly, thereby letting you pick the most appropriate one for each chakra.

A wise tip is to put a grounding stone such as smoky quartz in between your client's feet. This stone will serve as a powerful anchor for the treatment. Another tip is to start the session by placing the stones on your client's lowest chakra. You can then move up then continue doing the Reiki session.

In terms of removing the crystals, make sure to go for the one placed at the highest chakra. The last stone to remove should be the one in the lowest part.

## Recommended Crystals and Stones for Reiki Healing

*For the Root Chakra:* Stones that are red, brown and black in color. The best choices would be red calcite, onyx, black tourmaline, jet and obsidian.

*For the Sacral Chakra:* Orange or red stones including orange calcite, moonstone and Carnelian.

*For the Solar Plexus:* Yellow stones such as yellow calcite, golden topaz and jasper.

*For the Heart Chakra:* Pink or green stones including rose quartz, emerald, green calcite and jade.

*For the Throat Chakra:* Blue stones. A few examples would be blue opal, chrysocola and Lapiz Lazuli.

*For the Third Eye Chakra:* Stones with indigo color including amethyst, sugalite and purple flourite.

*For the Crown Chakra:* Purple, gold or white stones. Examples include diamond, amethyst, snow quartz, amber and cactus quartz.

# Chapter 10: Strengthening Reiki Energy

The Reiki practice does not stop after acquiring your desired flow of energy. You need to work on it consistently to ensure that the acquired energy remains strong. It is also important to note that the success, value and strength of each Reiki treatment rely on strictly observing simple, yet effective guidelines. Also, keep in mind that Reiki features the loving wisdom and energy of the most superior spiritual power.

You can receive a consistent and limitless supply of such energy and power if you just practice a few tips in strengthening Reiki energy. Some of the tips and techniques designed to boost and strengthen Reiki energy are the following:

## Take a shower or bath

Water has a lot of vital elements that can help in balancing your internal and external chakras. Some practitioners observed that not taking their daily shower makes it harder for them to activate Reiki. It is crucial to note that water is a vital part in a person's life. Aside from improving your hygiene, using water to clean yourself up also works in clearing blockages in your chakras and balancing them.

## Exercise regularly

Strengthening your acquired Reiki energy is also possible with regular exercise. You can expect the energy to flow more naturally if you spend time stretching, doing some cardio, weight lifting or performing any other physical activities before a Reiki session. You will also find it rewarding if you perform your regular workouts after undergoing a self-treatment through Reiki.

## Practice Reiki when your stomach is still empty

Solar plexus refers to the chakra that controls or regulates your digestive system. It is better to align all your chakras and allow them to focus on absorbing the Reiki energy and letting it flow smoothly in different parts of your body. While this is unnecessary, most practitioners say that it is better to get such alignment in chakras and prevent any potential distraction to the solar plexus. This can help the chakra to work even more effectively when it comes to supplying your body with the right level of energy to digest food. It also creates a better and smoother flow of energy.

## Expose yourself to the sun

If you want each Reiki session to produce your desired results, then getting ample sun exposure can help you a lot. As a natural source of light, the sun provides a powerful force that can help open up your crown chakra. The good thing about having an open crown chakra is that it stimulates the smooth flow of energy.

## Choose to perform the Reiki session in a warm room

If you are living in a place with a cold climate, then your best friend once you decide to perform Reiki is a space heater. Note that cold hands and feet may stop or block the flow of energy. In case you do not have a warm room or heater, then consider wearing thick wool socks and gloves.

## Get rid of all unwanted or negative thoughts from your mind

To strengthen your Reiki energy, it is best to clear your mind of all negative thoughts such as your worries and doubts. This can help you in activating Reiki and your intentions for practicing it. Note that you will never obtain the best results from Reiki if you allow negative thoughts to cloud your mind and vision. Clear your mind and breathe deeply. It also helps to say some affirmations or mantras during the session.

## Visualize the flow of energy

Reiki energy have the ability of flowing around and through you. It would be helpful if you direct this flow beginning from the crown, to the root then back up to the palm chakra. You may also direct it starting from the crown chakra straight to the palm. Imagine the energy that you get from Reiki as having a golden glow.

Some practitioners even claim that they visualize the energy to have the colors of the rainbow. While there are no specifics as to the color that one can assign to Reiki energy, you can choose to visualize your own depending on the situation. This is a huge help in allowing Reiki to work in your favor.

## Practice slow and deep breathing

As covered in one of the chapters of this book, your breathing patterns contribute a lot in achieving success in Reiki. Practicing the right breathing techniques can help you relax while also increasing your awareness about your intuition. This can further guide you all throughout the Reiki session.

## Play soothing music

Playing soothing music is an effective way to interact with and strengthen Reiki energy. Play music when practicing Reiki and let it flow through you while meshing with the energy.

## Be patient

There are instances when Reiki energy flows at a very slow pace especially if you constantly change positions or locations. There are times when you need to wait for a few minutes to feel the energy working. This is the main reason why you have to be patient in each session. Give the Reiki energy enough time to flow through you.

# Chapter 11: Reiki in Everyday Life

Applying Reiki into your daily life can work wonders in improving the quality of your life. Aside from being a relaxing and soothing practice, Reiki can also help improve your health by dealing with certain health issues caused by stress and a blocked and imbalanced chakra.

With the help of Reiki, you can tap into an unlimited source of energy, thereby allowing it to work wonders for your health and well-being. This chapter will help you apply Reiki in your daily life once you are able to attune it.

## Protect yourself through Reiki

It is no longer a secret that the world is an immense place. To help you deal with the struggles and challenges in this huge place, you should consider developing a protective shield. This is something that you can get from Reiki. Use Reiki in such a way that it acts as an invisible protective shield that prevents energetic debris from harming you.

You can practice Reiki every day so that it will serve as a psychic and emotional sponge for you. By protecting yourself through Reiki energy, you will have an easier time moving on and doing your regular activities.

## Practice Reiki every morning

Whether your energy is dwindling because you are not naturally active in the morning or because you spent the whole night partying and enjoying yourself, it helps to boost your energy in the morning through Reiki. Boosting your energy by practicing Reiki a few minutes after waking up can help improve your focus all throughout the day.

A wise tip is to visualize Reiki symbols when performing yoga every morning. It also helps to do the visualization when you are doing intense yoga positions that may cause you to want to give up. This can motivate you to continue with your yoga session no matter how difficult it is.

## Apply Reiki even on the foods you eat

It is also possible to send over Reiki energy to your meals to obtain the most nutrients from them. This is also beneficial if you want to shield yourself from harmful additives like added hormones and fillers in foods. This does not take a lot of your time every day. All you have to do is to hold your hands with your palms facing down above the foods. Send Reiki energy through this position.

## Apply Reiki in the workplace

The workplace is one of the most stressful environments that a person has to deal with. This could be due to a challenging co-worker, chaotic work schedule or temperamental boss. The good news is that it is now possible for you to reduce the stress in your workplace through Reiki.

Shield yourself by allowing the Reiki energy to flow smoothly through you. You can also shield other people around you by helping them calm down and keeping negative energy away from them.

# Conclusion

Thank you again for downloading this book!

I hope this book was able to help you learn the art of practicing Reiki and its many benefits. This book covers most of the things that you need to do about this traditional yet effective healing technique. You learned about its benefits, principles, its relationship to your chakras and some techniques to implement it to your daily life, including the use of deep breathing techniques and crystals.

The next step is to put the Reiki knowledge that you acquired from this book to practice. Start practicing Reiki with this book as your guide so you can begin enjoying its many benefits including increased energy, improved health and higher confidence and self-esteem.

Finally, if you enjoyed this book, please take the time to share your thoughts and post a review on Amazon. It'd be greatly appreciated!

Thank you and good luck!

Made in the USA
Lexington, KY
29 September 2015